Karen,
use the information
given to you in Dreams
heigs Joan

Dreamer's Handbook

And Diary

by Joan Arlin Hibbs

Joan Arlin Hibbs

Special thanks to the members of the

Beautiful Dreamers Dream Interpretation Group

Sierra Vista, Arizona

March 1991

Susan1, Susan2, Virginia, Jane, Joanette and Joan

and

Deep appreciation to my excellent editor,

Joanna M. DeRungs

Introduction

"What if you slept? And what if, in your sleep, you dreamed? And what if, in your dream, you went to heaven and there plucked a strange and beautiful flower? And what if, when you awoke, you had the flower in your hand? Ah, what then?" Samuel Taylor Coleridge

It is said that the dreamer's dream is truly a teaching theater of the soul. It is a place where lessons and experiences may be presented in an all-inclusive form and without harm to anyone. It is the personal center where the dreamer is the creator and the creations.

One of the most productive and easiest gateways to one's inner life is through the dream door. This exceptional tool, thus far mostly untouched, is perhaps the most customized personal view into ones inner conflicts, lessons and prejudices and is readily available to each of us.

In the dream state, the daily conscious mind is resting and that part of us connected to the Divine is fully awakened. If we are listening, our dreams will direct our life lessons and open doors to enlightenment.

If you are interested in the more scientific data compiled about dreams, we recommend you read the research information supplied at the end of this booklet found in Wikipedia.

This handbook is intended only to assist the dreamer who already values the dream and does not require a great deal of scientific authority.

Section One

 When taking up the study of dreams, it is often useful to have a group with whom to share and review the dream content. You may select a few people with whom you feel less stress and more compatibility. Then set a regular meeting time, place, and day. You might prefer a more loosely structured get together, meeting only when someone has a dream she wishes to present for group review.

 If your dreams have captured your attention for some time; if you are keeping a dream if you want to use your dreams but cannot remember them; then perhaps this handbook can be of service. Dream recall habits can be acquired.

Perhaps you would like to use the art of dreaming with your immediate family. A family dream group is quite useful and can create strong bonds within the family unit.

Families have a great deal to learn from and about each other. Dreams are a way for a family to communicate on a more spiritual level. Dreams are most useful if someone is unable to find the needed words to clarify then heal misunderstandings.

One must be prepared to accept anything the dream offers. Often the dream will deal with the daily business of living but eventually the practice dreamer will discover many facets of dreams dealing with as many as 10 to 15 different types of dreams. Since the dreams are contained within the dreamer's mind, it is a safe way to explore the wide-ranging levels of you.

When one is ready, the dream will present vital information or lessons and do so exclusively at the dreamer's timing and pace. When you are open, the dreams will come with the precise information. They will come when you can manage what they offer. You may expect repeat dreams, patterns of dreams, and an exciting variety of dreams – all designed to assist you in your daily life and spiritual development.

Every dreamer will have his or her own dream language. Some of us dream in color – some do not. Some of us dream in puns, some in the elaborate symbols. With diligence and a little patience, the dream will give forth its treasure trove of information. It will help you to begin by learning your unique symbols and style. If you discover an informative meaning to your dream, you will feel a sense of acceptance and recognition – even excitement – as a dream message is revealed.

If someone offers a translation or symbol interpretation that is not feeling comfortable, keep searching. If the dream causes confusion, keep on looking. If the dream is like a piece of the puzzle that does not fit, explore the idea that you might have it in the wrong classification.

If all else fails, ask for a clear answer in a dream just before you fall asleep.

Section Two

Dreams are a spiritual teaching method best when one is free of the physical laws and distractions. The mind and soul are free to create an experience anything.

The theater of the mind is completely within the dreamer and without anyone else involved. Thus, the play, the stage, and the experiences are entirely of the dream.

The types of dreams are many – here are a few. Feel free to add more if you discover them.

1. **<u>Challenge dream.</u>** A dream given to face a fear. It is to assist with breaking old barriers – to become free of a dreaded happening. Flying, dying, public speaking, loss of a loved one, feeling unprepared for some event, fear of ridicule, your fear of failure, etc. Dreams can allow the dreamer to experience the feared experience and may actually change the dreamer's attitude and vanquish the fear.

2. **Resolve a problem or conflict** This dream allows the creative self to review options or choices and allows each result to be known so any final action is the best possible choice. It is like a presentation of multiple choices acted out for the benefit of the dreamer. Thus, the desired outcome is known to the dreamer, as is the path. This might also be called the question-and-answer dream. Ask questions before going to sleep. Keep paper and pen by your bed. Answers come.

3. **Entertainment or recreation dream**. It occurs as a source of relaxation or relief, especially when one is engaged in intense daily living situations with little or no relief. The dreamer can create a way to relax during sleep. Dream visit to the islands, a playground or the experience daily life as a comedy or enjoy the wonderful feeling of floating and being very carefree. Dream vacations provide greatly needed relief time usually not scheduled into the overly busy life.

4. **Alert or warning dreams**. It is often regarding an undesired event that is about to happen, if the course of the actor (dreamer) does not change. Something in the physical life is being warned about. It might be a death, a car accident, failing health or a disaster of some sort. On occasion, it can also be a pleasant encouragement to stay on course. It comes at a time of great importance, to influence decisions affecting the dreamer's future. These dreams tell the dreamer how to avoid something or continue on a path. Alert dreams are not to be confused with prophetic dreams.

5. **Prophetic dreams.** Similar to warning dreams. These are quite often accurate in detail of an event in the future that will take place. It is wise for the dreamer to record and date these carefully in order to identify them in the future. In some cases, these dreams are given to allow the dreamer to intervene or prepare for an event of which the dreamer is completely unaware. The events might occur in a month, but can be as much as two years ahead of the event. The prophetic dreams seem to be rare. They often they go unrecorded and are never validated. Perhaps the best evidence of prophetic dream is the déjà vu, a feeling of having experienced something before, although in fact it is the first time that this has happened or been experience. Keep a detailed dream record to test prophetic dreams accuracy.

6. **Environmental dreams**. A dream may be in response to physical environmental influences. If the sleeping room is cold, the dreamer dreams she is in a snowstorm and so on. The dreams after eating pizza – often a cause for indigestion – might bring dreams about being taken to the hospital for stomach surgery or might cause idiotic, nonsense dreams, a dream completely unrelated to anything reasonable or logical it can be analyzed for insightful meaning.

7. **Spiritual reckoning dreams.** This series of dreams can start when we are very young. These dreams might appear as a series of falling, flying, loose teeth, or monster type dreams. Most everyone experiences these dreams that are, in truth, voices from ones spirit calling attention to the growth pattern, a phase, a need to move, change course or speed up or even to face a disturbing fear or hurt. The purpose is to point out the process of the soul development. Like everything in nature, the soul or spirit is on the course of growth to a given level of maturity. The spiritual dreams require attention at an early age. Few are aware of the importance of these spiritual knowledge dreams.

8. **Process report card dreams**. These are a sort of readout on the select quality of one's present activities. They come from the inner higher self. These dreams are given to encourage or discourage a particular way of life. One usually confuses these report dreams with warning dreams. They differ in that the warning is prior to serious choice times and the progress report is about the result of choices and paths already taken. They come in response to the dreamer asking, "How am I doing?"

9. **Daily conflict and Problem resolution dreams**.
These dreams– without other participant's physical
involvement – come to the dreamer with solutions.
The dream can offer options – a way of accepting
that which cannot change and still must be faced. It
can also offer a way to deal with an impossible
situation – a boss who is pressing too hard – you
can dream he dies or you leave the company.
Neither has actually occurred but the dreamer
experiences the temporary feelings while keeping a
safe distance and detachment allowing review of the
various responses and outcomes. The dreamer can
go on with life after learning from the lesson
presented in the dream play. One may leave the
impossible situation and gain permanent relief if
the lesson is finished and if leaving is truly the
better choice.

10. **Physical activity recreation or relief.** These include sexual release, blind person seeing, physically handicapped walking, or running again. These dreams meet a need of the body without any guilt or physical change or involvement of others.

11. **Visitation dreams**. Dreams experienced in mind-to-mind or heart-to-heart meeting. Someone, living or dead, visits with the dreamer or the dreamer visits another person, living or dead. This often occurs after the death of a loved one – often on significant dates or during tribulations. These dreams have significant difference from other dreams. They are stripped of personality trappings and are more spiritually focused. Love surrounds all beings. Joyfulness is present in each one. The exchanges are insightful and welcome. Words might not be spoken however, communication occurs.

12. **Personal out of body travel dream.** Just as it sounds, the soul travels to places near and far and seems to observe rather than interact with dream participants. One feels light as a feather and flies it treetop level enjoying the sights. Soul visits to home happen.

13. **Spiritual instruction dreams.** Spiritual teachers often show themselves in dreams and continue to teach us in a regular dream series. Some of these teachers are with this for life; others come only for a few sessions. The teacher must be invited; the dreamer must be open to this kind of communication.

14. **Spiritual dream work.** When we are separated from those whom we feel need assistance, we are able to be in touch with them, comfort and help heal them. Some teachers do all of their work in dreams and help others in dire need or when they are crossing over to a nonphysical body.

15. **Creative dreams**. These are identified when artistic or scientific work etc. is actually planned or executed. When awake, the dreamer will actually create the work of art, formula, or invention- as seen in the dream.

William Blake, The Land of Dreams "*The general function of dreams is to try to restore psychological balance by producing dream material that re-establishes, in a subtle way, the total psychic equilibrium.*"

Section Three
<u>Dream Group Guidelines</u>

1. **<u>Confidentiality</u>**. Each member must promise and give complete confidentiality. No member may share another members dream or revelations without the member's permission. One may share one's own dreams and analysis as desired. Some groups do not want their meeting place or membership known. Comply with the wishes of the majority in this matter.

2. **Commitment.** Each member must commit to keeping a dream log. It is best to date each entry. It is helpful to jot down a few of the daily living conditions and circumstances – much like a journal. Note the moon phases, food eaten, moods, cycles, and what you are experiencing that might contribute to the dream content. Include elements of television programs that appear in the dream a day or two following the program. Ask yourself why you are having this dream now, especially if the dream is not easily translated. Also, note symbols and instant dream interpretations. The weather and date give documentation to the dream if it is prophetic.

3. **Log detail.** Log as much dream detail as possible. Draw any object or place if you can. State colors, setting, people, ages of people and identify or name the person in the dream if that person is known. Note any symbol, feelings – during the dream and after – and notice if the lighting is bright or dark. The more detailed the better.

4. **Book selection.** The group might like to select one book about dreams. Each member should read it prior to beginning the group sessions. It helps focus the mind and give a group a commonly shared dream language and background. A dream book list is available near the back of the book.

5. **Honest Sharing.** Each group member should be encouraged to give and receive honesty. One must be willing to accept and not judge anything presented in a dream. It is important to form an atmosphere free of fear, rejection or shame.

6. **Acceptance.** Dreams brought before the group must be accepted by all group members as valuable information for growth, insight, and personal spiritual development. All members should be considered as equals, each one is both the teacher and student at the same time. It is best if there is not a set religion our church affiliation required of the members.

7. **Meetings.** Uninterrupted weekly meetings for the first month or two are comfortable. If the group does not meet in the summer, be sure each member keeps up their dream log. In a group member has an urgent need to have group help with the dream, a spontaneous meeting can be called at the request of a member. A phone conference may be used, if the gathering is not possible.

8. **Group size.** A good group number is somewhere between three and five. This smaller number allows more time for each dream. A session is usually more than an hour and less than four hours.

9. **Process.** The process: each member with the dream tells the dream, allows questions from members, and then hears each member's ideas about that dream – what it means, where it is classified etc. The dreamer is the only one to select the final meaning of the dream, incorporating the ideas presented and/or only their own instincts.

10. **Meeting place.** Meeting should not be in a public place. Members might take turns hosting sessions or one member might host all of the meetings. Atmosphere is important, so be sure the surroundings are pleasant, physically and emotionally safe, and comfortable. Meeting date should be by all members unless illness, vacation, or work interferes.

11. **Outcome.** The dream group can be a joyful and supportive experience while rapidly learning about the spiritual self and the personal self.

Section Four

<u>Here are the things you will need:</u>

1. **<u>Research.</u>** Read a few books about dreams to focus your thinking on dreams. Research dreams on the net. Settle on one book as the group's key book.

2. **<u>Suggestions.</u>** Give yourself suggestions. It is best to tell yourself you want to remember a dream just as you are dropping off to sleep. If you visualize yourself waking and remembering a dream, that might also help.

3. **Notations.** Place a notepad and pen by your bed so you can jot down a word or two to trigger dream recall. Give the dream a title. If you rouse from a dream, stay still until you have recalled the dream content. Sometimes it is best not to open your eyes, speak, or move until the dream is brought to the conscious mind.

4. **Title the Dream.** Once remembered, try giving the dream a title to help you recall it. Keep it simple. A dream about fighting with the monkey might be titled monkey fight.

5. **Awareness.** Acknowledge the urge within all of us to grow both physically and spiritually. Although dreams can be a great source of entertainment and relief, the dedicated dreamer will discover far greater riches.

6 **Trust dreams.** Trust that your dreams are just that - your dreams. Dreams are communications with your inner-self, higher-self and the entire collective consciousness. Therefore, dreams will not encourage or give permission to harm others or yourself. However, you might dream of an experience of harming or being harmed just to gain insight to the outcome of such ideas or actions. These actions of harm are not under any circumstances to be carried out.

7. **Records.** To keep dream logs that are more accurate record the date, the weather, moon phases and the key events happening in your life.

Listed below are a few interesting books about dreams:

Dreams by Larry Kettlekamp. This is the dream book available in school and public libraries for junior high school ages. It provides an introductory overview to the field emphasizing historical and scientific information. Published by William Morrow and Company, New York 1968. Be sure to look for used books on Amazon for a good bargain.

The Complete Dream Book, second edition by Gillian Holloway

Dreams: Clear Penny – New age dream stories with interpretations. Paperback by Mary Belle Claude.

The Everything Dreams Book: What you dreams mean and how they affect your everyday life. Everything from philosophy to spirituality by Jenni Kosarin.

The Complete Idiot's Guide Dream Directory. Paperback by Eve Adamson.

"Your dreams are for your exclusive use. You might change your behavior or habits because of a dream. Trust that only loving acts are encouraged – anything that encourages unloving acts are not spiritual lessons or guidance but perhaps merely a harmless working through a fear or anger.

If when we dream we are the dream and all things in that dream, could we be God's dream? Then is God all things and all things God?" Joan Arlin Hibbs

Suggested reading from Wikipedia:

The following excerpts are from the scientific research published in Wikipedia.

Neurology of dreams. There is no universally agreed biological definition of dreaming. General observations show that dreams are strongly associated with rapid eye movement REM sleep, during which an electroencephalogram shows brain activity to be most like wakefulness.

Stages of sleep. When the body decides that it is time to sleep, neurons near the eyes begin to send signals throughout the body. According to Jay Alan Hobson, these neurons are located in such close proximity to neurons that control eyelid muscles that the eyelids began to grow heavy.

During sleep. The body passes through five different stages, each differing in length and degree of sleep. Rapid eye movement sleep is when the majority of dreams take place. Dreams tend to last for the entire REM cycle ranging from about 10 to 25 minutes. Dreams usually occur during these regular sleep cycles, but they may also occur at other times such as when one falls asleep or begins to awaken.

In 1976, J. Allen Hobson and Robert McCarly proposed a new theory that changed dream research, challenging the previously held Freudian view of dreams as subconscious wishes to be interpreted.

Continual activation theory. Combining Hobson's activation synthesis hypotheses with Solms findings, the continual – activation theory of dreaming presented by Jie Zhang proposes that dreaming is a result of brain activation and sentences; at the same time, dreaming and REM sleep are controlled by different grade mechanism.

Dreams and memory. Eugene Tarnow, 2008, suggests that dreams are ever present excitations of long-term memory, even during waking life. The strangeness of dreams is due to the format of long-term memory, reminiscent of other findings that electrical excitations of the cortex give rise to experiences similar to dreams.

Hippocampus and memory. A 2001 study showed evidence that logical locations, characters, and dream flow may help the brain strengthen the linking and consolidation of somatic memories. These conditions may occur because, during REM sleep, the flow of information between the hippocampus and then neo-cortex is reduced. Increasing levels of the stress hormone Cortisol late in sleep causes this decreased communication.

Functions of dreams. There are many hypotheses about the function of dreams. Freud proposed that one function of dreams is to protect our sleep. However, the mind will awaken an individual if they are in danger or if trained to respond to certain sounds, such as a baby cry. Dreams may also allow the repressed parts of the mind to be satisfied through fantasy while keeping the conscious mind from thoughts that would suddenly cause one to awaken from shock.

Jung suggested that dreams might compensate for one-sided attitudes held in waking consciousness. Ferenczi propose that the dream, when told, may communicate something that is not being said out right. There have also been an analogies made with the cleaning operations of computers when they are off-line. Dreams may remove parasitic nodes and other "junk" from the mind during sleep. Dreams may also create new ideas to generation of random thought mutations. Some of these may be rejected by the mind as useless, while others may seem to be valuable and retained.

History of dreams. Dreams have a long history both as a subject of conjecture and as a source of inspiration throughout their history. People have sought meaning to dreams or divination through dreams. Jacob's dream of a ladder of Angels is one such dream.

Dream content. From the 1940s to 1985 Calvin S Hall collected more than 50,000 dream reports at Western reserve University in 1966, Hall and then the Van De Castle publish *The Content of Analysis of Dreams* in which they outline decoding system to study 1000 dream reports from college students. It was found that people all over the world dream of most of the same things.

Emotions. The most common emotion experienced in a dream is anxiety. Negative emotions are more common than positive feelings.

Gender differences. It is believed that in men dream an average of 70% of the characters are other men, while a female dreams contain an equal number of men and women. Men generally had feelings that are more aggressive in their dreams and women, and children dreams did not have very much aggression until they reach teens.

Sexual content. The Hall data analysis shows that sexual dreams show up no more than 10% of the time and are more prevalent in young two mid-teens. Another study showed that 8% of men and women's dream have sexual content.

Recurring dreams. While the content of most dreams is dreamt only once, many people experience reoccurring dreams – that is, the same dream narrative is experienced over different occasions of sleep. Up to 70% of females and 65% of males report recurrent dreams.

Common themes. Content-analysis studies have identified common reported themes in dreams. These include situations relating to school, being chased, running slowly in place, sexual experiences, falling, arriving too late, a person now live being dead, teeth falling out, flying, embarrassing moments, failing an examination, or car accident. In addition, only 12% of the people dream in black and white.

Dream interpretation. Both Sigmund Freud and Karl young identified dreams as an interaction between this unconscious and conscious. They also assert that the unconscious is the dominant force of the dreams and in dreams; it conveys its own mental activity to the perceptive faculty. While Freud felt that there was an active censorship against the unconscious even during sleep. Jung argued that the dreams bizarre quality is an efficient language, comparable to poetry and uniquely capable of revealing the underlying meaning.

Fritz Perls presented his theory of dreams as part of the holistic nature of Gestalt therapy. Dreams are seen as projection of parts of the self that have been ignored, rejected, or suppressed.

The other associated phenomena:

Lucid dreaming is the conscious perception of one's state while dreaming. In this state, a person can have control over characters in the dream as well as the dreamer's own actions. The occurrence of lucid dreaming has been scientifically verified.

Dreams of absent minded transgression. DAMT are dreams wherein the dreamers absentmindedly performs an action that he or she has been trying to stop an example is trying to quit smoking and dreams of lighting a cigarette. Subjects who have had the DAMT have reported waking with intense feeling of guilt.

Dreaming, a skeptical argument. Dreams can link to actual sensations, such as the incorporation of environmental sounds into dreams, or dreaming of urination while wetting the bed.

Recalling dreams. The recall of dreams is extremely variable, though it is a skill that can be trained. Dreams that are difficult to recall may be characterized by relatively little affect, and factors such as salience, arousal and interference play a role in dream recall. A dream journal can be used to assess dream recall for psychotherapy or entertainment purposes.

Déjà vu. The theory of déjà vu dealing with dream indicates that the feeling of having previously seen or experienced something could be attributed to having dreamt about a similar situation or place, and or getting about it until one seems to be mysteriously reminded of the situation or place while awake.

Dream incorporation. In one use of the term, "dream incorporation" is a phenomenon whereby an external stimulus, usually in auditory one, becomes a part of a dream, eventually than awakening the dreamer. This is a famous painting by Salvador Dali that depicts this concept, titled "Dream Caused by the Flight of the Bee Around the Pomegranate a Second Before Awakening."

The term "dream incorporation" is also used in research examining the degree to which preceding daytime events become elements of a dream. Recent studies suggest that events in the day immediately preceding and those about a week before, have the most influence.

Edgar Allan Poe, A Dream Within a Dream "*Dreams are more real than reality itself, they are closer to the self.*"

2013 Further reading:

Condron, Barbara (1994). The Dreamer's Dictionary. School of Metaphysics Publishing.

Crisp, Tony (2002). Dream Dictionary: An A to Z Guide to Understanding Your Unconscious Mind. ISBN 0-440-23707-6

Freud, Sigmund (1980). The Interpretation of Dreams, Avon.

Guiley, Rosemary Ellen (1995). The Encyclopedia of Dreams. ISBN 0-425-14788-6

Hadfield, J. A. (1954). "Dreams and Nightmares", Penguin.

Jung, Carl (1964). "Man and His Symbols", Doubleday.

MacKenzie, Norman (1989). "Dreams and Dreaming", Bloomsbury Books.

Van de Castle, Robert (1994). "Our Dreaming Mind", Aquarian.

"*I dream, therefore I exist.*"
Walt Disney, Sleeping Beauty.

Dream Diary Notes

Date_____ Day of the week

Weather _____

Phase of the moon_____

Physical condition_____

Dream Title_____

Dream Type_____

Your feeling upon awakening_

Dream setting_____

Your part in the dream_____

What is happening in the dream

Who else is in the dream_____

Color or black-and-white dream

Other dream detail_____

Why this dream now_____

Discovered meaning _____

Sweet Dreams .....

Made in the USA
Monee, IL
30 July 2023

40151165R00036